Home
com
ing

Elfie Shiosaki is a Noongar and Yawuru writer. She is a Lecturer in Indigenous Rights at the School of Indigenous Studies at the University of Western Australia, and an Editor of Indigenous Writing at *Westerly*.

Home com ing

ELFIE SHIOSAKI

Magabala Books

This is a Magabala Book

LEADING PUBLISHER OF ABORIGINAL AND
TORRES STRAIT ISLANDER STORYTELLERS.
CHANGING THE WORLD, ONE STORY AT A TIME.

First published 2021
Magabala Books Aboriginal Corporation
1 Bagot Street, Broome, Western Australia
Website: www.magabala.com
Email: sales@magabala.com

Magabala Books receives financial assistance from the Commonwealth Government through the Australia Council, its arts advisory body. The State of Western Australia has made an investment in this project through the Department of Local Government, Sport and Cultural Industries. Magabala Books would like to acknowledge the generous support of the Shire of Broome, Western Australia.

Magabala Books is Australia's only independent Aboriginal and Torres Strait Islander publishing house. Magabala Books acknowledges the Traditional Owners of the Country on which we live and work. We recognise the unbroken connection to traditional lands, waters and cultures. Through what we publish, we honour all our Elders, peoples and stories, past, present and future.

Cover Design Jo Hunt
Cover Image Getty Images
Typeset by Post Pre-press Group
Printed and bound by Griffin Press, South Australia

ISBN (Print) 978-1-925768-94-7
ISBN (ePUB) 978-1-925768-97-8
ISBN (ePDF) 978-1-925768-96-1

 A catalogue record for this book is available from the National Library of Australia

 Department of Local Government, Sport and Cultural Industries GOVERNMENT OF WESTERN AUSTRALIA

 Shire of Broome people · place · prosperity

Australian Government

 Australia Council for the Arts

This text includes the reproduction of archival material. Readers are advised that this material contains historical terminology when referring to Aboriginal and Torres Strait Islander people.

Contents

Introduction

Four generations of Noongar women in this story. I am the sixth.

Mattalan belonged to the ancestral waterways of her Wilman moort in the south west of Australia. She lived in an old Wilman world, before wadjela came.

Her daughter, Mary Alice Harris, also belonged to Wilman waterways. She created new bidis between many worlds with cultural fluency, and seemingly fearless advocacy for Noongar women's human rights. The Harris family, together with many other Noongar families, campaigned for decades against the *Aborigines Act 1905*, and the forcible removal of Aboriginal children. In 1926, Mary's brothers, William and Edward Harris, contributed to the establishment of the Native Union, the first Aboriginal political organisation in Western Australia.

Mary's niece, my great-grandmother Olive Amelia Harris, belonged to the ancestral waterways of her Whadjuk moort and mother, Alice Wilkes. She spent her childhood at Carrolup River and Moore River native settlements. Her father, Edward Harris, corresponded with the Chief Protector of Aborigines, A O Neville, for more than a decade, pleading for the return of his children. Olive lived displacement, seeking refuge with Wilman and Wajarri moort, and in Aboriginal bush camps throughout Mid West and Pilbara regions.

My grandmother, Helen Amelia Joseph, is Olive's daughter. I honour her strength, courage and resilience.

Our grandmothers' stories teach us about Aboriginal women's ways of being in our many worlds. Some of the stories in this collection are held in spoken histories, others in archival material, recontextualised with living katitjin. Some are held in my imagination. They are fragments of the many stars in my grandmothers' constellations. I track my grandmothers' stars to find my bidi home.

worl moorart djinda
sky full of stars

      boodjak birniny bidi
      carves track into land

ngany koort koorliny karlup
my heart comes home

resist

Story Tree

crushed underfoot
vibration travels
heel to heart

trace your remnant veins   skin
imprint your bones
into my hands

breathe you in

precious debris

bury you
under our story tree
trunk and branches   cry out

I was born in Perth   somewhere
my father   was up in Onslow   working on the jetty
my mother   was in Perth

there was a ship that took my mother down to Fremantle
it was called the *Amelia*
so I called myself   Olive Amelia

when my mother died
I was only eight months old
I was sent to a home

I remember sitting   in a cot
I sat there
nobody got up to lift me out of it   just sat there

it was a tin place
there were bunks
right up the wall

all the girls slept in the bunks
only me and Edna   we were too little
we couldn't get up into the bunks

that place was called Duhli Gunyah

---

* Olive Harris, recorded storytelling, 1994.

4

the people who used to live around there
                        I asked them what my mother was like

they said she had beautiful red hair

* Olive Harris, recorded storytelling, 1994.

I didn't know when I was born
                                    so in a way

I am not eighty-four
                        see?

* Olive Harris, recorded storytelling, 1994.

we were always hungry

                    there wasn't much

but I didn't mind

I liked it there

---

* Olive Harris, recorded storytelling, 1994.

my sister left

when I had measles
she sent back some vegies and a bag of potatoes

they said   Olive get up
your brother and sister are coming

* Olive Harris, recorded storytelling, 1994.

my head could just go over the table

she was making bread
I'd say   I'd like to help you   can I help you?
she would say no   you are too small

Mrs Floyd
                    I remember her name

* Olive Harris, recorded storytelling, 1994.

they would shave us
with a big horse machine

you could feel it   hot   going over your head
your hair was just   tight   to your skin

baldy, that was in Carrolup

---

* Olive Harris, recorded storytelling, 1994.

the girls used to sing
they had beautiful voices

every night the girls sang 'Gentle Jesus'
knelt by the bed

Mr Black was a very strict Christian

---

* Olive Harris, recorded storytelling, 1994.

I am anxious to have my children   home   with me
Grace and Olive   from Duhli Gunyah
Lyndon   from Carrolup

in order to have them with me
I have done what you thought necessary

increased wages
a suitable place to live in

the conditions under which they would be living
would be the same as any ordinary working man's home

---

* Edward Harris, Letter to Chief Protector of Aborigines, A O Neville, 31 December
  1918.

but this I must say

in all my dealings with you
I have never found you   sympathetic

how one sided and biased you are
I don't know whether you are trying to victimise me or not
              but it looks very much like it

I don't think I have said anything "out of place"
only what any father would say
              when he finds one so hard to deal with, like
              yourself
                  unsympathetic

on top of all this   you are a father yourself
and should understand the feelings of one

now   bringing this letter to a close
I appeal to you to have my children placed in my care
                  to remind you   I am their father

if you cannot do that
I'll try some other means to have my children restored to me
                  either through the press or a court of justice

an early reply to this letter will oblige

---

* Edward Harris, Letter to A O Neville, 9 March 1918.

Coorinja Dec 31st
1918

The Chief Protector
Perth

Sir
I am ancious to have my children home with me. Grace & Olive from Dulhi Gunyah, or Lyndon from Carrolup. In order to have them with me. I have done what you thought was necessary. viz a place with increased wages or a suitable place to live in. I would like to mention the conditions under which they would be living would be the same as in any ordinary working mans home, for anything further I would refer you to Mr J. S. Milne Guildford the gentleman whose I am working for

your faithfully
E. Harris
c/o. The manager
Coorinja Vineyard –
Toodyay

Image 1 Edward Harris letter, retraced by author

a fine day
a fine day
a fine day
a fine day
a fine day
a fine day
a fine day
a fine day
a fine day
a fine day

Image 2 Olive Harris handwriting, retraced by author

15

I can never convince myself you are anxious for me to have my
    children back

I have told you before that you are   hostile and biased
                       I still believe you are the same

in all my dealings with you re the children
you have raised   too many obstacles
                    created   too many difficulties

the result to me has always been   disappointment

I have carried out all the conditions you have imposed on me

I expect you to fulfil your promises

---

* Edward Harris, Letter to A O Neville, 29 March 1919.

Rain Will Come

The dry of the Wheatbelt rose from the horizon, chalky layers of pastel yellows, oranges and pinks uprooting the heat from the earth. Koorlang tracked towards the river with the other girls, away from the cool shade of the salmon gums. They sang 'Gentle Jesus' in chorus with the kulbardi watching over them like they were soft grey feathered chicks. The water pooled around imprints of Koorlang's small feet along the riverbank, forming silty clouds in the sand. The river shimmered in admiration of the children, treasuring the gift of their Sunday afternoon fellowship, and the stolen times they stopped by on their way home from school. Koorlang waded out into the river and dipped her head under the water, ritually cleansing herself of heat, sweat and dust. She drew a deep breath and, wriggling her toes into the river sand, dove into the deepest pool of water. Its coolness kissed her sunburnt cheeks. Koorlang closed her eyes and dreamed the river in, made herself a dusk offering.

The sunlight of tomorrow will warm the surface of the water, make her molecules speed up and move so rapidly that, tightly packed and vibrating against each other, she will escape into vapour, leaving behind the salt from the tributary. Suspended in air, rising high into the atmosphere, she will cool down again and condense. Returning to water, she will gather to form clouds and precipitation, drifting over the Darling Ranges towards the Indian Ocean.

She will then fall from the clouds, out of the afternoon sky, in droplets of rain, filled with rays of sunlight and a million rainbows. Returning colour to her mother's boodja, the place she belongs to.

there was a river on our way to school
we used to wrap a water snake around a tree
leave him
he would be still there   when we came back

one day, we did that
when we came back
                    he wasn't there

* Olive Harris, recorded storytelling, 1994.

Blood Dreaming

I

Overheated, Koorlang closed her small eyes, searching for Walyalup. Dreaming the southerly into her lungs, its saltiness into her bloodstream.

She hadn't felt the southerly on her skin for months now, caressing her neck with her hair, whispering into her ear. Cooing over her with Ngangk.

No sound of voices, or sight of faces, for two days now.

Except hers.

Koorlang had hit her, the nurse. Hit her right in the face. She was wearing glasses, too, and shards of a broken lens cut deeply into her cheek.

The nurse had hit her first.

That morning Koorlang refused to go to school with the other children. She was shame. She couldn't even look at the nurse. Her small head shaved, cut and bleeding from the horse clippers biting at her scalp.

The nurse dragged Koorlang though the courtyard of dirt and eucalypt debris, her small feet raking over a game of hopscotch. She pushed her into the darkness inside the small iron shed, her thick fingers struggling to close the lock.

III

Koorlang's skin searched for the southerly's draft inside the boob. Sitting on the sandy floor, her bony knees dug into her chest. The iron door softly framed by the light of midday. Yet, holding the darkness in.

V

In the darkness, without windows or natural light, Koorlang closed her eyes.

Dreaming the time when the southerly became a draft, the sun fell into the Indian Ocean and the stars rose into the night's sky. Her sky full of stars.

When her bed was soft with gullee needles and warmed by kangaroo skin. When her young mind was quietened by the night song of the djiti djiti in the full moon. When it was soothed by the smoke of the campfire and the crack of its embers.

When the warmth of Ngangk's body next to hers drew all the chill out of this world.

Reborn

if I could take you from that place
                    I would

if I could hold you in my arms
                    I would

reborn
as mine

comfort you
always

just as
your own mother   wanted to

I have applied to Mr Neville more times than I should have
each time   he has refused my request

several times   I have asked him on what grounds does he refuse
    to restore my children to me
                        I am still in the dark

of course   I will apply again for my children
also ask for an inquiry

the way I have been treated by that gentleman
                        is an outrage to one's feelings and affections

his inclinations to thwart me in this matter
have been successful thus far

wartime conditions and other matters prevented me having my
    case tried   so far
but I am still going to go on

                    hope for justice in the finish

_____

* Edward Harris, Letter to Deputy Chief Protector of Aborigines, 29 March 1920.

you speak of doing the best in the interests of my children
                    I cannot see it

your past actions show
                    you are malicious

you have never missed an opportunity
                    of hurting me

not once

also   you have used your position as Protector and the Aboriginal Act

                    to gratify your malice

I have more to say
                    later on

---

* Edward Harris, Letter to A O Neville, 21 August 1920.

Sir

pain
suffering
heartbreak
distress
desperation
grief
sorrow
anger
frustration
pleading
begging
game playing
false representations
subversion
protest

Yours Faithfully

Grandfather

my grandmother told me
her grandfather was a dignified man
he believed all people were equal

and he was equal to any other person

before me is a copy of the Aborigines Act
I have no hesitation in saying

         it is a foul blot

      on the State of Western Australia

a disgrace

         to those formulating such Acts
     also to the members of Parliament who were responsible for such
       Acts becoming law

I am certain the majority of the people in this State
have no idea   how cruelly the natives are treated

        that they are outlaws

      that without doing anything

        forfeit their rights to live in freedom in their own land

they can be taken from any part of the State
compelled to live in prison
on reserves

why make Pariahs of natives in their own land?
people with the civilisation of yesterday
struggling midst adverse conditions

if the aborigines must go under

then for humanity's sake

give him a fair deal

while he is still   on the surface

* William Harris, Letter to the Editor, *West Australian*, 25 September 1925.

for hundreds of years
in song and story

it has been Britain's boast
under her flag was found justice and fair dealing for all

but in dealing with the aborigines
it has been reserved for Western Australia to overturn British Law and Justice

ever since the whites settled in Western Australia
the aborigines have not lived in a more cruel and lawless state

their condition has gone from bad to worse

and has now become unbearable

---

* William Harris, Letter to the Editor, *Sunday Times*, 14 November 1926.

the department established to protect us

is cleaning us up

under the present Act

Mr Neville owns us

body   and soul

---

* William Harris, 'Black Man's Burden', *West Australian*, 10 March 1928.

Image 3 Olive Harris, undated, painting on paperbark

Venus

My grandmother's eyes dance as she tells me this story.

When her mother was a young woman, she would meet her white friends at Cottesloe Beach. She was a cosmopolitan young woman, seemingly at ease in the many worlds she moved in and out of. Cottesloe was the playground of bright young things in the 1920s. In the evenings, the Indiana Tea House would host dances, cabarets with live jazz bands, or silent films on its lawns.

They would picnic in the shade of the Norfolk Island pines and swim in the turquoise waters of the Indian Ocean. Her friends called her 'Venus' in her swimsuit, my grandmother tells me. Venus is the Roman goddess of love and beauty – and victory.

These were moments of great happiness and excitement, she tells me. Listening to her story, I remember the special kind of excitement only girls on the cusp of womanhood feel. When her body can no longer contain her elation, and she feels like she might just burst.

I do not find this story about my great-grandmother enjoying the excitement of her youth in the archive. A story that makes my grandmother's eyes dance when she tells it to me. These are some of the years of my great-grandmother's life when she evaded the surveillance of the government.

When she cannot be found in the archive.

This story tells me something about the way my great-grandmother represented herself. That she was a cosmopolitan woman. That she was confident. That she was daring. That she was admired by her friends.

The archive could never hold the beauty of a daring Noongar woman.

Tidal Race

seas of remembering forgetting   even reimagining
collide and converge in archival memory
unceasing battle of oceanic giants

forming waves
whirlpools
                    turbulent currents

no beacon
warns and guides us
around the watery battle ground

I give myself   to the sea

in those three years
Mum disappeared
from the Welfare
old Neville   somehow

there weren't many reports on her
actually there were none
she kind of just ran off
disappeared   for a while

she worked for some good people
one was a Jewish lady
a seamstress
made her lovely clothes

she had lots of non-Aboriginal friends in Perth   that she told me
they used to call her Miss Venus
reckoned she was so beautiful
                        in a bathing suit

* Helen Shiosaki, recorded storytelling, 2017.

18.7.27 left Perth for Toodyay where she will take up residence with her father who stated that he would find suitable employment for her in the District: 21.10.29 Advised by Northam Police that Olive is now working for Mrs. Ann Hancock, Northam: Wages 15/-d. direct to the girl: 27.5.30 Advised by Northam Police that Olive had left Mrs. Hancock's employ several months previously and obtained work from Mrs. Fred Roe who found her unsuitable: He also advised Olive was seeking employment and was at present residing with Mrs. James Howard, Northam: 19.6.30 Olive taken by Edward Harris, her father, to his home at Toodyay: 29.12.30 Report from Northam Police that Olive is now residing at 3 Richardson St., South Perth with her aunt Miss M. A. Harris: Prior to that she had been working for a Mrs. Snowball, Commercial Bank, Northam for about two months: 19.1.31 Report from South Perth Police to the effect that Olive is engaged as a domestic at Mrs. McMullins', Angelo St., South Perth: 9.4.31 Located working for Mrs. A. F. Stowe, Suburban Road, South Perth: Wages 15/-d. per week: Ceased with Mrs. Stowe (date unknown): 9.7.31 Advised that Olive is living with her aunt, Miss Harris at South Perth, and has been getting occasional work from Mrs. Higgins of South Perth: 4.8.31 Olive took up residence at the Girls' Home to await employment: 21.8.31 Entered service at Mrs. D. Lindau, Mukinbudin: Wages to be 7/6d. per week, 2/6d. to Olive and 5/-d. to Dept. for banking: 18.9.31 Ceased with Mrs. Lindau and returned to Perth: 23.9.31 Commenced with Miss Wineberg, Chelmsford Road, North Perth: Wages to be 10/-d. per week, 5/- to Dept. and 5/- to girl: 21.11.31 Ceased with Miss Wineberg: 8.1.32 Entered services of Mrs. Barr Goyder,

Peppermint Grove: Wages 12/6d. per week, 5/-d. to Olive and 7/6d. to Dept. for banking: 11.2.32 Ceased in this employment: 23.9.32 Employed by Mrs. F. Lewes. 1 Norfolk St, North Perth. Wages 5/- p.w. and keep:

---

* Olive Harris, Personal history card, Aborigines Department.

inflicted
by savage   brutish dogs

in the shape of white men

on helpless men and women and children   in their power

the hunting
of men   like wild beasts

the barbarous
flogging   of the slaves

the chaining
of untried   prisoners

the brutal lust
which respects

neither wife

nor mother

nor daughter

can you wonder   then

why the blacks don't love the whites?

* William Harris, Letter to the Editor, *Sunday Times*, 24 April 1904.

the indenture system
the cause of nearly all the natives'

miseries

the devilish legal instrument
enables savage lustful squatters and their henchmen

to practice abominable cruelties

enslavements

lusts

it is nothing but legalised slavery
I don't see how it could be called anything else

under it
the squatter gets all

the native nothing

except tucker

and brutality

the Department
might as well not exist

run more as a blanket
to cover   unknown deeds   of inhuman whites

---

* William Harris, Letter to the Editor, *Sunday Times*, 24 April 1904.

when I had my little daughter
she couldn't come out

Matron pressed on my stomach
then she came out

her name was Helen
born at North Fremantle

having a baby hurt that much
but I thought it was my punishment

my baby Helen

                    look at her now
              she is a lovely thing

---

* Olive Harris, recorded storytelling, 1994.

had to earn their keep
Mum didn't talk much about it

                        but she did say

scrubbing floors   on her knees
how her back used to hurt

---

* Helen Shiosaki, recorded storytelling, 2017.

after I was born
Mum more or less escaped from the home with me

got on a train
she was that scared of someone seeing me

it was Stolen Generation   too

little babies being taken

from everywhere

* Helen Shiosaki, recorded storytelling, 2017.

Mum told me he was a very kind man
but she never ever spoke much about him   at all
she was supposed to meet up with my dad

but he never turned up

she never talks much about those things

* Helen Shiosaki, recorded storytelling, 2017.

from there

        Mum was that scared

Welfare would have known then
        that I was born
they knew
they would be looking for me

so she decided to go up north   Mid West
where she had some family

---

* Helen Shiosaki, recorded storytelling, 2017.

Legacy

that time
he broke me

            into uncountable pieces

I dreamed
your strength

to piece myself
back together

            bit by bit

Blood Love

I

Koorlang took her first breath of salty air on the verandah of Hillcrest Maternity Hospital in Walyalup.

That day, it was too cold to be outside on the verandah. Koorlang didn't have a bed, a warm blanket even. But nestled underneath her mother's woollen winter coat, she was lulled into unguarded sleep by the patterned rhythm of Ngangk's heartbeat.

Hillcrest was a hospital for the newest wards of the state. But Koorlang didn't belong there. She belonged to the place where the beeliar snaked into the Indian Ocean, where the sun rose over the hills and fell into the water.

There, underneath Ngangk's coat, Koorlang had everything she needed.

Ngangk love.

Mother love.

Blood love.

II

The southerly carried echoes of old voices as it swept across the verandah, welcoming Koorlang into this world. Its cold gusts scattered cloudy thoughts far from Ngangk's mind. Even though she had given birth only hours ago, she tenderly hid Koorlang underneath her coat and left Hillcrest. Her steps were frantic, but determined, as she felt the southerly gently nudging her along her path.

Ngangk hurriedly boarded the tram from North Fremantle to the city. There was no safe harbour for her in this port. She was on her way to meet Koorlang's father. They wanted to get married and be a family, the three of them. As the tramline traced the Indian Ocean coastline, electric blue in shallow waters sent lively currents into her heart.

Ngangk imagined a new world for her first child. In this world, children would know who they were and where they came from, so they could always find their way home.

III

Koorlang's father never turned up.

Ngangk flattened her palm against her mouth to stifle a thick sob rising in her throat. There was no time. She knew she needed to keep moving and find her way home.

Ngangk jumped trains from Perth to Morawa with Koorlang still hidden underneath her coat. Holding together against the swaying of the back carriage, Koorlang and Ngangk rattled through damp fields of oat and wheat planted after the first rainfall of autumn. Ngangk didn't belong to this place, but she had spent her childhood at Mogumber and learned to walk its tracks.

That night, family welcomed Koorlang and Ngangk into their home. They had a warm bed and blanket. They had a place to rest, nurture and grow. They had a place to hide out for a fleeting childhood.

V

Koorlang grew up and learned to walk these tracks, her small footprints burying Ngangk's own deeper into the jam soil.

Ten years passed before time stood still and Koorlang was taken to a cold unfeeling place without Ngangk love.

Koorlang came to know that this old world loved and hated in tenacious equal measure. On that first day, shielded by Ngangk's own body, she had known only love.

Starry

I hold on to this sadness

to tell your story

if I let it go

I lose you

my sky full of stars

Wanting

sometimes I feel your steadying presence

when I do
I close my eyes

you would have loved this
you would have loved being here
                    right now
          with me

my skin would have shimmered with your admiration
my body   warmed by your pride

wanting you here

I go along thinking
             this is what you would do
      or say
    or how you would be

but I never really know

I'm only guessing

survive

I can remember our first trip up north together
packs on our backs

I can remember the big red dust road we travelled on
gone on forever   cogla trees on the side of the road

of course I would have been carried
but I can remember   saying I wanted to walk   I can walk!

I was so independent

going so far
then jumping trains

that's how we moved from one town to the other

---

* Helen Shiosaki, recorded storytelling, 2017.

we didn't even own a clock
                    we didn't own much at all

all we owned   we carried on our back

                    nothing else

_____

* Helen Shiosaki, recorded storytelling, 2017.

Mum listened to classical music at night
the farmer lent us a radio

we listened with her
telling us how beautiful music was

even though we were living in a camp
                    we listened to classical music

even though her life was so hard
                    she still had that beauty of music

that stuck with me forever

we were in bed
when that radio was playing

---

* Helen Shiosaki, recorded storytelling, 2017.

Wandoo Whistling

Dad got a job on a farm around Morawa
circled by wandoo eucalypt
he used to make coal

there used to be this song
whenever I hear that song
I think of that time

just whistle while you work
and cheerfully together we can tidy up the place

cut down wandoo
dig into jam soil
ditch from shovel

set them alight
burning buried
under corrugated iron and soil

whistling as he bagged the coal
from the wandoo

this is a story about Jim I can tell you

Dad ploughed up the ground
he used big draught horses
every night   he had big coppers boiling

the first thing he did was bring the horses in
take off their harnesses
all the horses smelling like sweat   white foam on them

he'd get soap
rinse them down   with lovely hot water
soap them up

rinse them off
dry them

                really dry them

then he'd put salve on
where the harnesses used to go

he used to complain about the farmer
not looking after the horses   well enough

that's a strong memory

                he was very kind

---

* Helen Shiosaki, recorded storytelling, 2017.

Mum and Dad had to go out on this farm
clear the land for cultivation

they left me behind

I remember screaming and running after them
then they'd bring me back again

then I'd break away again
run and scream after them

about three times
until I was too exhausted

                    and I accepted

                being left behind

it was traumatic

it was terrible
                        I'd never been left behind before

they left me with my mum's cousin

they lived in a house

it was the first house I'd ever been in

the house was furnished   with chairs   a table   beds
it had a clock a radio

I was in this room on my own
in this lovely   big   soft   bed

I was so unhappy

as if I was deserted

all I could hear was this ticking of this clock

to this day I can still remember this
ticking of that clock

I don't know how long I was there for
jobs weren't long term

a couple of weeks here
a couple of weeks there

you travelled

         all the time

* Helen Shiosaki, recorded storytelling, 2017.

up to the Goldfields
panning gold
finding as much to survive

if you didn't find gold   you didn't have food

pan for it
little specks
in a metal vial

one day   I spilt it
all the gold in the vial
after they'd worked so hard to get so much

my mum shouted at me
I was so scared
                              I ran

I wasn't far from the railway track
I got on that track
                              never stopped

as fast as I could

Mum chased me   for a while
then my uncle he chased me
brought me back

by the time I got back
Mum must have been feeling sorry for me
she gave me a big hug

said   it was alright
they'd try hard
pan for a bit more gold

when there wasn't gold to help with food
shopkeepers used to throw out the stale vegies
sprouted onions and potatoes

pick all the best ones
fry them up in fat
make a big damper

---

* Helen Shiosaki, recorded storytelling, 2017.

Blood Instinct

I

Their camp was in darkness, except for the glow of embers in the fire. Gullee needles quilted Koorlang's flour bag mattress and kangaroo skin warmed her small body in the coldness. Their camp was in silence, except for the intermittent lullaby of a kulbardi stirring.

Ngangk shook Koorlang from her dreams when she saw the headlights cutting through the wandoo on the road to the farm in Walkaway.

II

Ngangk took Koorlang's small hand in her own and they ran towards thick fields overflowing with ripened Geraldton Smoothskin tomatoes. Ngangk stopped, her strong arms lifting Koorlang up, and cradling her as she ran again. Koorlang was half-asleep, dreaming about swimming in rock pools of Coronation Beach the day before, and wading out onto the fringe reef at low tide to hunt crayfish.

Ngangk and Koorlang pressed themselves into the loamy soil of the field, underneath the cherry-red vines. Ngangk's heartbeat blocked Koorlang's ears from the sound of heavy boots, the breaking of vines with a wooden baton and the crushing of leaves underfoot.

The light from torches danced on top of the vines, as if the stars had fallen out of the sky, dusting Ngangk and Koorlang with eternal luminescence.

III

As the footsteps became louder, Ngangk covered Koorlang with her woollen winter coat, tucking her golden red curls in. Koorlang was too small to know this game. All she knew was that she must be so still, so quiet, make herself so small, smaller than the white dots in the night sky.

The policeman called out, "just a gin".

Koorlang pressed her small cheek deeper into the sandy clay soil.

IV

The night sky of the Mid West blanketed the field, like its own kangaroo skin. Koorlang peeked up, to find weitch nesting on his green eggs in the Milky Way. She closed her eyes, dreaming the time she and Ngangk had tracked into the bush in the middle of the night, away from their campfire at Gascoyne River. Kneeling beside her, Koorlang had followed the tip of Ngangk's index finger up into the sky. The wonder. That weitch had been there all the time, watching over her sleeping.

Koorlang opened her eyes to the clanging of handcuffs and the thud of the car door. Ngangk was gone. Wheels kicked up gravel and dust settled over the field. She opened her eyes and searched for the hay shed where she had played hide and seek with the other children camping at the farm.

She played this game with Ngangk, too, hiding until she came back to find her.

people were so proud

they lived in hard conditions

yet   they were very proud people

they tried   their very best

---

* Helen Shiosaki, recorded storytelling, 2017.

that was the school I went to
for the very first time in Mullewa

I remember the teacher putting me up on the table
saying to the other children

just look at Helen

she's an Aboriginal

look how clean she is

                        that was very embarrassing for me

            I look back on it now

        I don't feel very good about myself

to be me
to be put up on that table

everyone's looking at me
everyone's saying how clean I was

for an Aboriginal

* Helen Shiosaki, recorded storytelling, 2017.

when we had our sandwiches at school
we had damper
                       butter if we were lucky
            and tomato sauce

Charlie and I used to go hide   in a corner

the other kids used to have these big thick   lamb   sandwiches

one of the kids followed us
he said   what are you having?
we showed him what we were having
                       and he said   can I have a taste?

we felt so ashamed

we said   ok

then he wanted to swap
once he had tasted the damper
                  and the butter
            and the tomato sauce

he wanted to change us for the big meat sandwiches

that's what we used to do
swap damper for the sandwiches

we never had bread
to have bread
you had to have money   in your hand   all the time
                    because you had to buy bread every day

---

* Helen Shiosaki, recorded storytelling, 2017.

the town people
complained about the Aboriginal people
                          living on the outskirts of town   in Mullewa

Welfare decided to send them all to the Common
up from the big wheat silos in town
had to go through a big creek   to get there

when you had those big rains
water just rolled down that big creek
people couldn't get across to buy food   until the water subsided

the government gave people tin   to build humpies
put a windmill up there   for water
where they were supposed to have their camps

once there was a big wind   big rain
knocked down everybody's makeshift camps
everybody got wet   headed for the racecourse   big sheltered sheds

                          it was a terrible experience

                          all cold and shivering

after that time I don't think a lot of people rebuilt their camps
they ventured back into town
                to the outskirts

* Helen Shiosaki, recorded storytelling, 2017.

Not Equal

not equal, she said

her eyes left mine
retreating into herself

                              not treated equally, she said

correcting herself
teaching me
always

my little sister Connie was born at the Common   in Mullewa
I was about four

all I can remember   was this little girl
running around among the big trees   black hair   curls

all you could see was this lovely little thing
                              running around with curly black hair

everybody used to make a fuss   of her

everybody loved   this little child

she was only about eleven months old when she died

I remember them saying

                    how hard it was to get across that creek

          to get into town

to buy food

or medicine

                                                                    .

———————————
* Helen Shiosaki, recorded storytelling, 2017.

when my little sister Connie died
Mum had a little locket

one little snip of her hair

she really treasured it

* Helen Shiosaki, recorded storytelling, 2017.

I suffered when I had my children

I suffered for my little girl Connie
only to lose her after

she was a lovely little thing
                         she never used to cry

there were other Connies in the family

my sister Connie

and Robert called his daughter Connie

* Olive Harris, recorded storytelling, 1994.

when Robert was born, I was eight

it was a house
but some of the rooms were dirt floor
the kitchen area was a wooden floor

my mum had Robert in this little room
with a dirt floor
an iron bed   a single bed

we were going to school at that time in Perenjori
I said   I've just had a baby brother
they wanted to see him

we were the only Aboriginal kids at the school

there were no other Aboriginal kids

they came in

I said   all our furniture's put away
it's in another room
we haven't got it out yet

because I was
even at that age
I was very self-conscious   and proud

about these bare rooms
with nothing in them
apart from this single iron bed

Mum was lying there
with the baby
they were all making a fuss of the baby, Robert

* Helen Shiosaki, recorded storytelling, 2017.

I never used to go to the doctor when I was carrying
                            people didn't want you to stay in the hospital

I had to sleep on the verandah

* Olive Harris, recorded storytelling, 1994.

this girl and this baby
come from one of the farms
the baby was sick
we went to the hospital
but the hospital wouldn't accept us

they wouldn't accept Aboriginals

we went home
back to our house   in Moora

the baby died in our house

                    Aboriginal people were treated differently

          always in your life   you were different

                    you weren't treated the same as everybody else

that was a traumatic experience

I was eleven
my brothers, too, would have experienced that   Charlie, Ray
    and Robert

it was done   all the time

I was born in North Fremantle in a hospital
Charlie was born in a camp
Connie was born in a camp
Ray was born in a camp
Robert happened to be in a half house
                  in a room   with a dirt floor   and a
                        single iron bed

later on when Mum had Max
the first child after the war
just as well she was accepted into hospital
a breech baby

if she was in the bush
or not accepted
                I don't know

               that's just how they were

just send you home

Not Equal

Not Treated Equally

Grandmother

Koorlang stood on the shore of the fringe reef at Coronation Beach, hopping from one small foot to the other. The southerly at midday was madly chopping the Indian Ocean, stinging her eyes with salty water. Her brothers waded out onto the reef, hunting crayfish in the rock pools at low tide. Her ears were burning from her uncles' stories about the poisonous spines of the cobblers on the reef.

Koorlang took her first unsteady steps onto the black jagged rocks. Always trying to keep up with the older boys and not be a girl. Never be a girl.

The choppy water clouded the reef at times. Koorlang fell hard into a rock pool, crying out. Her father, fifty metres out on the reef, looked back. "You right, bub. Walk it off", he called out to the horizon. This was her father's good remedy – for her bull ant bites from the banks of the Capel River, the burning of the back of her legs from the slide, and the time she fractured her right elbow falling off her brother's skateboard.

Koorlang bit down on her pink bottom lip to stop herself from crying. Blood pooled around the cuts on her knees. She lowered her head, black curls veiling her face, washing her scrapes in the salty water. She moped on the shoreline until her father came back, nets bursting with crayfish.

Home, Koorlang wrapped her small body around the trunk of her grandmother's leg. She held up her scraped palms and pouted her bottom lip at the same time. Then she lifted up her cut knees and pouted even harder. She didn't say anything. She didn't need to. Her grandmother knew.

Her grandmother cooed with the ocean of compassion she held in the vessels of her heart. She cared about even the smallest of scrapes, the ones dismissed by others who weren't moved in the same way she was.

Her grandmother gently cleaned the wound with the antiseptic from her nurse's bag, and when Koorlang cried, she blew on her skin to soothe the stinging. She placed an oversized gauze over the cut, to acknowledge that her pain mattered, she mattered.

Then, taking Koorlang into her strong arms, her grandmother squeezed her tight, the tightest Koorlang had ever been squeezed, "you right, bub".

The water in the pots began to simmer, ready for the crayfish. The table was set with jars of vinegar, loaves of white bread and butter, ready for the sweet meat. Their Christmas lunch.

When she was older, Koorlang would listen to her grandmother's stories about working as a nurse at the hospital in Mullewa, and how white people didn't want her to touch them. They didn't want to be skin-to-skin with the soothing, smooth hands that cared about even the smallest of scrapes, the hands her grandchildren treasured.

Image 4 Olive Harris, undated, painting on paperbark

that's when Jim was in the army

Jim left me with a one-week-old baby
he went
he volunteered to go

there I was
pushing the pram up the street in Perth with the kids
looking for a place

I got a place to live in Bayswater
I was frightened
no water

It was terrible on your own
                                with little ones

I was in a terrible way
but I had to do it
no help for me

_____

* Olive Harris, recorded storytelling, 1994.

when Dad went overseas
Mum moved to Perth to Bayswater

she was renting a little place on Beechboro Road
a little house

it had an air-raid shelter   dug out in the back   in a zigzag
it had a water pump

you get the wife's pension from the army
Mum got that

we used to go to school on the bus
tags around our necks   with our names on it

they used to have these big sirens   in case something happened
you'd be prepared for it at the school they had trenches

the siren would sound
the kids would get scared
                            thought these planes were coming   to bomb us

marching all in order into trenches   crouched down
just practising

when the sirens sounded, when we were home
Mum would panic
                        thought we were being attacked

I can still remember her   herding us into the shelter   at the
    back of the house
waiting until it was   all clear

an allotment

we didn't get good money
like the white people

twenty-two pounds for me
and the kids
for a fortnight

* Olive Harris, recorded storytelling, 1994.

hundreds out back
die   of starvation

without seeing

          tasting

the miserable dole

          they call Government Rations

* William Harris, Letter to the Editor, *Truth*, 30 July 1927.

I used to be by myself with the kids

I also looked after other kids
their father came to me   asked me

he said   I don't know what to do
so I said   alright

there were two boys and a little girl
I used to patch their pants to make them last

---

* Olive Harris, recorded storytelling, 1994.

I had golden red curly hair
everybody used to stop   make a fuss of me

one day somebody stopped me
wanted to give me two shillings

I was thinking   I would love two shillings

but I was too proud to take it

I said   no thank you

Mum always taught us manners

_____

* Helen Shiosaki, recorded storytelling, 2017.

all the kids used to come to my place
we lived next to a big park
I would put a big blanket down for them to sleep

poor little things
Ronnie was a sick little one
I couldn't say no to them kids

anything extra I would keep it for Ronnie
I'd say   no you kids
can't have this   it's for Ronnie

later on, when he was grown
he came straight up to me, when he saw me
he played the drums for the dances in Perth   the Coolbaroo Club

he had rheumatic fever

he died young

I used to do anything for kids

----

* Olive Harris, recorded storytelling, 1994.

Jim went overseas place   like Manila

he didn't get hit while he was away
he did get malaria, but
he had to have tablets

when he came back
I used to sit up all night with him
get hot feverish   then get cold

I used to have to make him warm

---

* Olive Harris, recorded storytelling, 1994.

I don't know what they gave him when he came back

he didn't come back home with anything

* Olive Harris, recorded storytelling, 1994.

I would remind Parliamentarians
and others who object to the half-castes having a vote

many of that despised class
fought in the Great War

now they are refused a vote
they are not allowed to enter a public house

even to take shelter from a storm

_____

* William Harris, Letter to the Editor, *West Australian*, 25 September 1925.

when Dad returned
he suffered from malaria fever   very badly

he was kind of traumatised
drinking much more heavily than he ever did

it affected him

I remember going to see him
laying in his bed   covered in sweat   shivering

they weren't recognised

they were supposed to have been given land
after they returned

somewhere in Perth
I really don't know   that's just what you hear

they would have seen awful things

he was in New Guinea   fighting the Japanese
he was so brave

a hand grenade was thrown
he picked it up   just ran

dived on the grenade
threw it as far as he could

it went off as soon as it was in the air
just bang

that's a story I heard

          but never ever spoke about the war
     very quiet about it

      very much alone

---

* Helen Shiosaki, recorded storytelling, 2017.

Australia's theirs

        their country

Aboriginal men are proud men

they wanted to protect

        their country

---

* Helen Shiosaki, recorded storytelling, 2017.

it broke down families

if you wanted your citizenship
                    you had to live like a white man
you couldn't mix up   with other Aboriginal people

it was very difficult

even though you got it
lived like a white man
you still weren't accepted

as far as everyone else was concerned

                    you were an Aboriginal

                    living in no man's land

I know from experience

when I was among some white people
I'd wish I was like them
just white

when I was among Aboriginals
I'd wish I was like them
I didn't want to be white

you just want to be accepted by everybody

renew

Lost in Archive

It never occurred to me
that I would find you
there

in that cold unfeeling place where you cried tears onto paper
that weighed so heavily on my heart   it slowed its beating

It never occurred to me
that you would take me into your arms   like I belonged to you
there

and you would warm my cold hands in between yours
bringing movement back to my numbed limbs

It never occurred to me
that you would speak to me
there

with that comforting voice of bed time stories and tucking in
and your words would breathe your life back into mine

my heart now beating in time
to a rhythm that was not its own

It never occurred to me
that you would find me
there

that I had been lost   not you
and you would take me home

The Gaze

looking directly into the face of it
I wanted to look away

I could feel the cold gaze
on my family

on me

                        its coldness crept into my own spirit

I am one
in a family
of half-castes

who had a mother [Mattalan]
                    worthy of the greatest love
            and respect

one who   in every way
easily reached

                    the white man's

            highest   and purest

            standard of morality

I am sure hundreds of half-castes can truthfully say the same for
    their mothers

_____

* William Harris, Letter to the Editor, *Sunday Times*, 8 January 1922.

Starstruck

The stars watched over Koorlang asleep in the camp grounds on the riverbank. Their hearts sang brightly with stellar spectra. A starstruck child. Always trying to keep her heavy eyes open and dream in their luminosity. Always restless with night minds.

Her mother instinctively pulled Koorlang into the curve of her side, warming her from the coldness carried in the westerly. Every night the stars awoke to dream with Koorlang, premonitions, her grandmother called them. They were as old as the universe, and knew every story that had come, and was to come. They searched the darkness for starstruck children to whisper their stories to, waves in space.

Koorlang had told her mother about a great white cloud over the horizon that would cover the sky, for a time, when she could no longer see weitch nesting on his green eggs in the Milky Way. Her grandmother had taught her to love weitch. Their life ways sustained one another. When Koorlang watched her father dance in the light of the campfire, arching his back, stamping his feet, curving his arms and hands into a long-necked beak, her own heart sang.

When Koorlang woke under the blanket of stars, she buried herself deeper into her mother's side and searched for weitch in the Milky Way. He was still there, watching over her sleep, always. She searched for the great cloud in her dreams and could not find it, but a coldness had entered her spirit, knowing it was to come. This coldness would never leave her, even when she would become a woman with children of her own. It would keep her body tense, her heart holding breath and skipping beats.

Koorlang sensed a time when the stars would stop singing, and boodja would fall silent. Yet, her heart was full of feverish hope she would be able to hold her family together in the silence. She would teach her grandchildren to love weitch, whether they could see him in the Milky Way or not.

Her Manifesto

Royal Commission on Treatment of Aboriginals

(a) Asiatics and undesirables should be excluded from native camps.

(b) Proximity of native camps to towns: I am of opinion that native camps should be a reasonable distance from towns.

(c), (d), (e) In cases of disease and illness hospitals could be erected and arranged in native villages and camps at the larger or main settlements. Such settlements should be extensive, containing suitable farming areas for general production that would provide occupation and become self-supporting.

(f) Aboriginals employed by any persons should have equal privileges as Europeans where their services are satisfactory.

(g) Education and training at mission settlement schools should include training of boys into agricultural pursuits, and to be generally useful, and general domestic household training for girls, besides being trained as nurses.

(h), (i) Aboriginals should be subject to the laws of this country similar to Europeans.

(j) In cases where the Aborigines Department hold monies or property in trust for children, those concerned should receive the same at the age of 21 years.

The necessity of the native having to be provided

with a permit to work and save his living is unjust and seriously objectionable.

I recommend the Aboriginals receive Parliamentary Representation.

Mary Alice Harris
March 28 1934

---

* Mary Alice Harris, Letter submitted to 1934 Moseley Commission, Con 987, Item H, SROWA.

unjust

and seriously objectionable

The Past is a Second Heartbeat

the timbre of her voice
broke the silence

                    fleeting tones

kick up dust
swirl around

particles settle
silence returns

but I can still feel the echo reverberating in my body like its
    second heartbeat

MARY ALICE HARRIS, Sworn and examined:

1380. BY THE COMMISSIONER: Why do you wish to give evidence?

– I don't know that I want to.

---

* Mary Alice Harris, Testimony to 1934 Moseley Commission, AN 537, Acc 2922, SROWA, pp. 464–6.

1385. You say undesirable persons should be excluded from native camps?

– Yes.

1387. And whom do you mean by undesirable persons?

– I have seen some white men there, going
back and forth.

* Mary Alice Harris, Testimony to 1934 Moseley Commission, AN 537, Acc 2922, SROWA, pp. 464–6.

1392. In this statement you refer to hospitals in camp. Would you have a hospital in every native camp?

– No, but I think there should be a collapsible hospital in a camp when necessary and that the girls should be taught nursing by a trained nurse. We used to get that sort of thing under the Imperial Government, before we had responsible government. If the girls were taught nursing they could always look after patients. Generally there is a doctor in every district and he could give advice to the girls who had been taught nursing.

1393. You suggest hospitals in native camps, but if the camp is close to a town any sick person can be removed to the hospital in the town?

– But natives like to be out by themselves.

---

* Mary Alice Harris, Testimony to 1934 Moseley Commission, AN 537, Acc 2922, SROWA, pp. 464–6.

1394. Then you say that aboriginals should have equal privileges with whites, what privileges?

– They should be paid wages as whites are.

1395. And what are they going to do with their money? Have you ever been in the far North and seen what is done there?

– Yes, I have seen native men go to the station and buy trousers and shirts for themselves and dress materials for their women folk.

1396. But the natives who work without wages get all things necessary from the stores?

– They should have their own money.

1397. What could they do with it?

– The same as white people.

If they are capable of doing the work they should be paid so that they could put their money in the bank.

---

* Mary Alice Harris, Testimony to 1934 Moseley Commission, AN 537, Acc 2922, SROWA, pp. 464–6.

Williams River

Stepping out into the morning sun, Koorlang stood on her South Perth verandah and felt the westerly wisp around her neck and whisper into her ear. She pulled the collar of her winter coat up around her cold ears. Closing her eyes, she turned her face eastward, like the flowers in her garden, waking and unfurling to the sun.

Yet, even in this sacred morning ritual, her heart was empty of hope, waiting. Always waiting, for justice.

This new world. A white world. A man's world. A world that spun on an axis of spitting, hateful greed. The rules of the wadjela game never fair, changed to guarantee she would lose, every time, no matter how skilfully she played.

Sitting down on the steps of the verandah, Koorlang hugged her shins and rested her cold cheek on her knees. The westerly caressed her face, its swirling hands soothing her like it would a child. It carried her away from the Indian Ocean and over the Darling Ranges, to dream her childhood and the time with her mother on the banks of Williams River.

This old world. A loving world. A woman's world. A world where the bond between mothers and children were never broken.

1399. You also suggest that aborigines should be subject to the laws of the country, just as are the Europeans. Do you mean all natives?

– Yes, everyone.

1400. How could you explain to them what the laws of the country were?

– A British Member of Parliament said that there should be the same law for white and black.

I also suggest that the Native Law should be taught, so that when a trial was taking place, someone could interpret the language and assist the jury.

---

* Mary Alice Harris, Testimony to 1934 Moseley Commission, AN 537, Acc 2922, SROWA, pp. 464–6.

1403. You also recommend that aborigines should have parliamentary representation. Do you want them to have the right to vote?

– Yes.

1404. Do you want one member for all of them?

– No, one in each district.

Natives are not represented in parliament now.

1405. Are you aware that this Commission is the outcome of representations made in parliament?

– Yes, I know.

---

* Mary Alice Harris, Testimony to 1934 Moseley Commission, AN 537, Acc 2922, SROWA, pp. 464–6.

Mary Alice

she made herself visible
for great consequence

                    in a world which made her invisible

writing on behalf of us
               Aboriginals and half castes
to have the existing law or Act
            abolished

that requires us to have a permit
to work
               In The Land Of Our Birth

I doubt if there are any original inhabitants
              whose land   like ours   taken over by the Britons
are required by the law of their government
           to have a permit   to work   In The Land Of Their
        Birth

we protest against the law
              applied by Chief Protector Neville
enforcing the law by sending a police officer
          in the case of Olive Harris

Olive is quite capable of taking care of herself

must we get advice From You the Minister for the Aboriginals Department
or shall we petition   His Excellency The Governor of Western Australia

to have that unjust law   abolished

Waiting A Reply

---

* Mary Alice Harris, Letter to the Chief Secretary, Norbert Keenan, 2 February 1931.

acting on the advice to go and interview the Premier Sir James Mitchell
    I called to see the Premier
        but could not see him.

I was advised by the Premier's private secretary to go and see you
        but the young lady in your office told me
            I was to see the Chief Protector Mr Neville first.

I called to see Mr Neville
    but found that he had gone on three weeks leave.

it seemed to me that day
    I had called on 3 Caesars
        but could not get any satisfaction.

---

* Mary Alice Harris, Letter to the Chief Secretary, Norbert Keenan, 2 February 1931.

Now

Mr Neville
he did
not know

the way
he looked
at her

           then

           determined

the way
we look
at him

           now

Heartsickness

man with   koort warra

strike my
cheek

strike me
from your

                 records

fill your   koort warra

with ink
from my

                 sword

cut out your   koort warra

poison seeps
from last beats

Dancing Devil

breath from our lungs
carries our life

                                our voice
outside ourselves

not apart

not unseen

not silent

rapid rising
shear in atmosphere
rushing in
dancing devil
kicking up dust

breathe us in

Which Way

Koorlang stepped out of the shade under the biboolborn circling the wetlands and into the sun. Her eyes traced the rays of sunlight diving into the shallow pools. A snake-necked turtle carrying an ancient moss forest on its back kissed the surface of the water and took a breath of damp earthy air.

Koorlang rolled up the legs of her jeans and waded out, kicking up generations of debris from the biboolborn, shedding its leaves and paperbark. Her grandmothers' voices swirled around her feet in clouds of silt, rising to the surface and revealing a thick forest of roots on the bottom. She knelt in the water, scooping leaves into her lap, gently cleansing the dirt from their blood lines. They whispered of the horror and the wonder, the delight and the misery. Her hands were muddied, and dirt stuck underneath her fingernails. Her heart caved in under its heaviness. The leaves floated on the surface in historic shades of emu-egg green, colouring its silty darkness.

Koorlang waded out deeper, the biboolborn singing out to her as the wind rustled in their branches. She dug her heels into the bank to stop herself falling down a very deep well. Velvety green flickered from the back of the turtle foraging in the debris at the bottom. She knelt, tilted her head back and baptised herself, until the sun lit up her own face under the water. The heavy weight in her heart floated to the surface. Her unburdened body sank deeper into the well, until its banks gently cradled her in loving arms. Black tresses of her hair tangled with the forest of roots until she could no longer move, her eyes becoming pools of water, her skin silt and her arms flowing currents. Unafraid, she remained still, not knowing which way was the light, and which way was the darkness.

Author's Note

First Nations storytelling recognises the human agencies of Aboriginal women to resist, survive and renew. We find freedom in storytelling, to restore humanity to our intergenerational story cycles, and carve bidis between ancient and new worlds.

I acknowledge my grandmother, Helen Shiosaki, as the custodian of the stories in this collection. I thank her for giving permission to share her and her mother's voices and stories. These stories, in writing, archival material and artwork, may not be shared without her permission. I acknowledge my father, Alf Shiosaki, for walking this katitjin bidi with me. I acknowledge Whadjuk Traditional Owner Len Collard for advising me about Noongar language.

Some of this research was supported by the Centre for Human Rights Education at Curtin University, where I held a position as an Indigenous Postdoctoral Research Fellow from 2015 to 2018. Some of these stories were developed in creative writing workshops with Linda Martin and Laura Keenan. Some of these stories have been published in *Westerly: Ancestors' Words* (Westerly 2019) and *Once: a selection of short short stories* (Night Parrot Press 2020).

I thank Rachel Bin Salleh and the team at Magabala Books, and editor Linda Martin, for nurturing the growth of this work. I also thank readers Catherine Noske and Nadia Rhook, for their fiercely nurturing spirits.

These stories reflect only the here and now in a long katitjin bidi ahead of learning about First Nations story work.

Noongar Word List

beeliar	river
biboolborn	paperbark
bidi	track, path
boodja	Country
djiti djiti	willy wagtail
gullee	sheoak
katitjin	knowledge
koorlang	child
kulbardi	magpie
moort	family
ngangk	mother; sun
wadjela	foreigner
weitch	emu

---

* This glossary has been developed in consultation with Whadjuk Traditional
Owner Len Collard, and a literature review of historical language databases in:
Whitehurst, R (compiler) 1992, *Noongar Dictionary: Noongar to English and English
to Noongar*, Noongar Language and Culture Centre (Aboriginal Corporation),
Bunbury; Bindon, P and Chadwick, R 1992, *A Nyoongar Wordlist from the South
West of Western Australia*, Western Australian Museum, Perth; Moore, G F (1842),
*A Descriptive Vocabulary of the Language in Common Use Amongst the Aborigines of
Western Australia*, Bradbury and Evans, London; Grey, G (1840), *A Vocabulary of the
Dialects of South West Australia*, G Norman, London.